Original title:
Crumpled Notes Beside the Dragon Hoop

Copyright © 2025 Swan Charm

Author: Olivia Orav

ISBN HARDBACK: 978-1-80562-019-8

ISBN PAPERBACK: 978-1-80563-540-6

Chronicles of the Inked Dragon

In shadows deep where whispers flow,
An inked dragon weaves tales of woe.
With scales of midnight, it soars on high,
Guarding secrets that never die.

Its breath ignites the night with fire,
Awakens dreams, sparks fierce desire.
A tapestry stitched from tales long gone,
In every stroke, the past lives on.

Through ancient forests, wild and free,
The dragon glides, a spirit's plea.
It churns the ink from time's own well,
In each adventure, a new spell.

With tales of love and loss entwined,
In every legend, the truth we find.
The ink drips slow, but never fades,
In the heart of those who seek the glades.

So heed the call of the inked beast,
For in its presence, we are released.
From silent pages, its stories sing,
A timeless bond, eternal spring.

Illuminated Fragments of the Past

In the corners of forgotten rooms,
Buried echoes wake from gloom.
Fragments glow with a golden light,
Whispers of days, lost in night.

Each flicker tells of laughter sweet,
Moments captured, bittersweet.
Through the dust, a tale appears,
Of love, of joy, of hidden fears.

With ink-stained hands, I trace each line,
Drawing forth the threads divine.
In shadows deep, the heart is laid,
Illuminated truth won't fade.

Time's mosaic, pieced with care,
Stories linger in the air.
Pieces dance in the twilight's glow,
Revealing paths we yearn to know.

So gather close, let us explore,
The heart of history, forevermore.
Within these fragments, wisdom waits,
Unlocking hearts and ancient gates.

The Alchemy of Written Echoes

In the depths of silence, words ignite,
A dance of letters, a quill takes flight.
Each stroke a potion, each phrase a spell,
Transforming the mundane to a tale to tell.

Golden ink flows on parchment's embrace,
Magic woven in each sacred place.
Echoes of whispers, timelines entwine,
Crafting worlds where the heart can shine.

Through valleys of dreams and mountains of lore,
The alchemist scribes, forever to soar.
In realms of the written, the soul finds home,
In echoes of echoes, forever to roam.

Shadows Encased in Fiery Essence

Beneath the moon's watch, shadows do flee,
Encased in embers, a flicker to see.
Twilight's embrace, a delicate waltz,
Where secrets awaken, lost in the pulse.

Fires of longing, in whispers they share,
With each crackle and pop, a promise laid bare.
Shadows entwined with the flame's golden glow,
Dance to the rhythm, a heartbeat in flow.

Cloaked in the night, they twirl and they spin,
Resilient, determined, like spirits within.
In the warmth of the blaze, they find their release,
In shadows encased, they discover their peace.

Whispers at the Threshold of Ashes

At the dawn of twilight, soft voices arise,
Whispers of spirits, where the silence sighs.
Between worlds they linger, a liminal space,
Dancing with echoes, a delicate grace.

Ashes of stories, remnants remain,
Each fervent ember, a touch of the flame.
A threshold of dreams where the past comes alive,
In whispers of shadows, the lost souls thrive.

From the depths of the fire, new life can bloom,
In the ashes of yesterday, hope finds its room.
So listen closely as night gently falls,
To the whispers of time, as the silence calls.

A Fable's Breath in Flame

In the heat of the moment, a fable takes flight,
Its breath made of fire, igniting the night.
Stories unspoken, yet vivid in glow,
Unraveling wonders where imaginations flow.

A flicker of wisdom, the heart's pure delight,
With each whispered tale, the shadows invite.
Through trials and triumphs, the heroes will rise,
In the dance of the flames, destiny ties.

For each fable's heartbeat, a lesson to share,
In the warmth of the fire, find kindness and care.
Fables breathe life, in the spark of their flame,
Transforming the world, forever remains.

Whispers of Forgotten Wishes

In twilight's hush, where echoes fade,
Dreams once bright, now softly laid.
A candle's flicker, shadows dance,
Lost hopes linger, in a trance.

Upon the breeze, a whispered plea,
For futures bright, what could be.
Stars align, in silent grace,
Each wish a glow, in timeless space.

The gentle night, a guardian true,
Holds secrets old, and tales anew.
Forgotten paths, where spirits roam,
A quest for hearts, to find their home.

But dreams can fade, like silken thread,
In gilded silence, the words unsaid.
Yet still they linger, in the air,
A tapestry woven, with love and care.

So listen close, as shadows weave,
And find the magic, if you believe.
For in the dark, your heart can see,
The whispers of what's meant to be.

Shadows of Inked Dreams

In pages worn, where secrets lie,
Ink drips slowly, 'neath the sky.
Each line a portal, a world anew,
With shadows danced, that beckon you.

Echoes of voices from ages past,
Stories etched, forever cast.
Within the margins, a fleeting sign,
Of hopes held close, in heart's design.

The quill's soft scratch, a serenade,
Of battles fought, and love displayed.
In whispered tales, the dreams take flight,
While shadows linger, in the night.

Beneath the stars, where wishes bloom,
Lies the essence of every room.
Ink and heart, forever entwined,
In shadows of dreams, let truth be defined.

So delve into the inked embrace,
And find your spirit, your own place.
For in the darkness, a beacon gleams,
A bridge of hope, in shadowed dreams.

Ephemeral Scribbles Under Moonlight

Beneath the silver, gentle glow,
Scribbles dance, as breezes flow.
Ephemeral thoughts, in quiet grace,
Whisper secrets, the night's embrace.

Moments fleeting, like stars that fade,
In twilight's grip, magic is made.
With every sigh, a story spun,
Under the watchful eye of the sun.

A hush of time, where magic stirs,
In scribbles soft, the heart concurs.
With ink of dreams, and moonlit glows,
The river of thought, endlessly flows.

In the canopy of the midnight air,
Each fleeting thought, a precious care.
For in the dark, our spirits roam,
In ephemeral verses, we call home.

So take a pen, and let it glide,
Let dreams unfurl, and hope your guide.
For every scribble, beneath the light,
Is a testament of heart, in flight.

The Secrets Beneath the Scaled Sky

Beneath the scales, the cosmos weep,
In whispers held, where shadows creep.
A tapestry sewn, of sun and storm,
With secrets wrapped, in celestial form.

The stars, like eyes, they watch and wait,
For dreams to rise, to celebrate.
A heartbeat echoes, in cosmic throng,
Of worlds uncharted, where hearts belong.

In whispered verses, the night unfolds,
Of ancient lore, and tales retold.
Each grain of stardust, a glimmer bright,
Bears witness to the dreams of night.

Through nights of terror, and days of light,
The scaled sky holds both dark and bright.
In every shadow, a spark ignites,
To paint the canvas of starry nights.

So look above, with hope in hand,
For the secrets whispered in the land.
In every twinkle, a promise lies,
In the vast expanse of the scaled skies.

Fables in Fragments

In shadows where whispers play,
Catch the tales of yesterday.
Fragments of dreams drift about,
In this world, filled with doubt.

The echoes of laughter fade,
While illusions gently invade.
Each story unfolds with grace,
Leaving behind a soft trace.

Beneath the moon's silver glow,
Hidden truths begin to show.
Fables written in the night,
Illuminated by starlight.

Words like feathers on the breeze,
Dance with a mystical ease.
In a garden of thought, we find,
Magic woven in the mind.

So gather the tales you keep,
In the corners where dreams seep.
Each fragment a treasure chest,
Waiting to reveal its best.

The Dust of Lost Words

In the corners of the page,
Lies a tale that's hard to gauge.
Words like shadows, thin and frail,
Whisper softly, yet they pale.

Dust collects on spoken dreams,
As silence drips from faded seams.
Echoes of voices long passed,
In the quiet, memories cast.

Each syllable holds a chance,
To revive a forgotten dance.
The dust, it sparkles like the stars,
Hiding stories behind bars.

In the stillness of the night,
Lost words find a flickering light.
They rise like smoke from the fire,
Carrying secrets and desire.

So gather round, and heed the call,
For stories are waiting to enthrall.
In the dust of lost words we find,
The magic of the heart and mind.

Scribbles under Fiery Wings

Beneath the sky, where embers glow,
Ideas take wing, and dreams bestow.
Scribbled thoughts across the night,
Flames of passion burning bright.

The whispers of dusk dance freely,
With ink that flows so deeply.
Underneath the fiery plume,
Creativity finds room.

Each stroke a burst of flight,
Carving tales in shadowed light.
Words flutter like butterflies,
Chasing down the starry skies.

In this realm of ink and flame,
Nothing ever feels the same.
Scribbles twirl and leap with glee,
Unfolding their wild mystery.

So let the wings of thought take soar,
To distant shores, forevermore.
In the scribbles, truth shall ring,
Underneath those fiery wings.

Secrets Written in Ash

Under the embers, tales reside,
In the ashes, mysteries hide.
Every flicker holds a key,
To a past we cannot see.

Wisps of smoke curl in the air,
Carrying whispers everywhere.
With every spark that disappears,
A secret buried, lost in years.

In the ruins of dreams once bright,
Ashes glow with a faint light.
What was lost can still regain,
In the silence, echoes remain.

So listen close, and you may hear,
The stories that come near.
Secrets woven in the past,
Through the ashes, always cast.

In this world where shadows play,
Lingers hope at the end of day.
For every ash bears witness true,
To the fires that shaped me and you.

Searing Glyphs on Weathered Paper

In the shadows of ancient lore,
Symbols dance, forevermore.
Ink spills tales of ages past,
Whispers of secrets, held steadfast.

Fingers trace the parchment's groove,
Echoes of thoughts that must not move.
Legends etched in fiery glow,
A tapestry of what we know.

Stains of passion, tears of dreams,
Crafted realms from silent screams.
Each curve a spell, each line a fight,
In the twilight, hearts ignite.

Crumpled edges, stories worn,
A fragile map of souls reborn.
Through the ages, ink shall flow,
Carving futures, seeds to sow.

Within these scripts, the truth shall lie,
A bridge between the earth and sky.
In twilight's grasp, the glyphs entwine,
Bound by magic, line by line.

Sovereign Ink upon Scales

Upon the dragon's mighty hide,
A tale of glory does abide.
Sovereign ink, a royal hue,
Paints the legacy of the true.

Every scale, a story's mark,
Of battles fought, of journeys stark.
With each stroke, a fierce decree,
Bound by the magic of the sea.

Legends whisper in the night,
Inky shadows, fierce and bright.
Chasing flames, where dreams take flight,
A sovereign's heart, aflame with light.

Glistening under moonlit skies,
The dragon soars, the spirit flies.
With scales adorned in tales of old,
An empire forged in whispers bold.

In the ink that never fades,
Resides the power, magic cascades.
A symbol of strength, forever true,
Sovereign ink, both fierce and blue.

A Symphony of Scorched Thoughts

Beneath the cinders, embers glow,
Whispers of dreams that ebb and flow.
In the chaos, melodies rise,
A symphony of scorched skies.

Notes of anguish, tunes of light,
Fleeting shadows in the night.
Each refrain, a spark, a flare,
Memory wrapped in smoky air.

Strings of hope, plucked with grace,
Resonate in time and space.
Harmonies born from ashes deep,
Awakening echoes that never sleep.

With every heartbeat, music swells,
In the silence, a tale compels.
Fragments sing of love and loss,
A symphony, a bittersweet gloss.

Eternal dance of fire and frost,
Giving voice to what was lost.
In the cacophony, find your part,
A symphony of the scorched heart.

Notes from the Edge of Fire

On the brink where chaos reigns,
Notes are scribbled, inked with pains.
From tongues of flame, ideas spark,
Lighting pathways through the dark.

Mysteries weave in flickering light,
Each letter borrows from the night.
In the heat, both fierce and bright,
Words take shape in desperate flight.

Quills of ember dance and play,
Scribing truths that must not sway.
A journal's heart, both wild and free,
Capturing flames of history.

Whispers carried on the breeze,
Notes of solace, memories seize.
In the winds, where passion swells,
Stories rise like ringing bells.

From the fire's kiss, wisdom grows,
What is feared, the heart now knows.
Notes from edges brave and stark,
Shine like stars against the dark.

The Dragon's Echoes in Paper

In a realm where whispers dwell,
Dragons crafted tales to tell.
Their roars in ink, bold and bright,
Echo through the endless night.

Feathered quills like scales did dance,
Scripted fables hold the chance.
To unravel secrets deep,
Woven in the dreams we keep.

Pages flutter like dragon wings,
Embers spark as memory sings.
Fragile parchment, brave and true,
Breathes in stories old and new.

Within each crease, a fire glows,
Tales of triumph, tales of woes.
In every line, a heartbeat missed,
By those who dared, by those who kissed.

So listen close, oh reader kind,
For dragons roam within your mind.
Let their echoes guide your night,
In the tales of paper light.

Frayed Edges of a Forbidden Tale

In shadows deep, a story lies,
Frayed edges whisper, softly sighs.
A spellbound heart, a hidden glance,
Forbidden love, a fateful chance.

Bound by parchment, secrets hold,
In verses thick, the truth unfolds.
Tattered dreams, with every breath,
Awakened whispers dance with death.

Ill-fated paths in twilight roam,
Calling souls who feel like home.
Beyond the bounds of fate's embrace,
They pen their sorrow, seek their grace.

Through cruel hands, the ink will bleed,
Yet hope ignites in every deed.
For in the night, the heart remembers,
The warmth of love through cold Novembers.

So turn the page, oh ageless lore,
Unlock the chains, and seek once more.
For in the fray of tales so bold,
Lies a truth that longs to be told.

Shadows of Ink on Fiery Breath

In shadows cast by flames so bright,
Ink flows swiftly, bold in flight.
A dragon's breath, both fierce and warm,
Shapes the world in magic's form.

Soft moonlight on a scroll does gleam,
Carrying forth the dreamer's theme.
With every stroke, the darkness swells,
As ancient stories weave their spells.

Fleeting echoes of yesteryears,
Drying ink and unshed tears.
Each word a spark, igniting fate,
In every line, the heart does wait.

Dragons glide on wings of lore,
Through realms where silence dares to soar.
With fiery breath and ink-stained claws,
They trace the line of hidden laws.

So linger here, in shadows' grip,
Where tales are born on sunlight's tip.
For in the dance of ink and fire,
Lies the essence of our desire.

Malachite Memories in Haste

In malachite, the past entwines,
Buried deep in ancient mines.
Each memory, a gem aglow,
Reflecting winds of long ago.

Haste forbids the tender care,
Yet whispers rise in fragrant air.
Stories shimmer, lost and found,
In every smile, a truth unbound.

Through verdant fields where time stands still,
Echoes linger, hearts to fill.
In every corner, shadows play,
While twilight kneels to bless the day.

So gather round, oh dreamers bright,
Embrace the dusk, revive the light.
For malachite holds tales untold,
Of love and loss, of brave and bold.

With every heartbeat, memories chase,
In a world that yearns for grace.
So write your fate in hues so bold,
And let your spirit dance, unfold.

Recording the Flight of Shadows

In whispers soft the shadows play,
Dancing lightly at the close of day.
Their secrets weave through twilight air,
A tapestry of dreams laid bare.

They flutter quick, elusive, free,
Sketching shapes that none can see.
A silent song, a fleeting flight,
Chasing stars in the cloak of night.

Each flicker holds a tale untold,
Of mysteries, both dark and bold.
With every turn, a story spun,
Beneath the watchful moon and sun.

The ink of night begins to dry,
As shadows blend with the midnight sky.
They vanish like a whispered breath,
Leaving behind a trace of death.

So heed the flight of shadows wide,
For in their dance, the truths may bide.
A dance of light, a fleeting dream,
Where nothing's ever as it seems.

Secrets of the Flame-Kissed

Amidst the embers, secrets dwell,
In fire's heart, where warmth compels.
The flames that flicker, rise and fall,
Whisper tales, both grand and small.

With every spark, a story gleams,
Of ancient kings and vibrant dreams.
The scent of ash fills evening air,
As shadows scatter everywhere.

The flame's embrace, a lover's touch,
Keeps hidden truths, we crave so much.
With golden hues, it paints the night,
Crafting worlds in its fleeting light.

Each flicker holds a memory tight,
A dance of hope, a fleeting plight.
In secrets kindled, hearts alight,
Finding solace in the night.

So gather 'round, let stories rise,
In flames of passion, wisdom lies.
For in the heat, we learn, explore,
The secrets whispered evermore.

Parchment Torn by Secrets of Old

In corners deep of a dusty tome,
Lies parchment worn, a tale of home.
With edges torn and ink that fades,
Whispers call through the ancient blades.

Each scribbled word, a riddle found,
In tales of magic, lost and bound.
The ink reveals what time has kept,
In shadows where the secrets slept.

A map of journeys, paths unknown,
A heart of courage, now overthrown.
What secrets wait in ink-stained grace,
Echoing softly, time to embrace.

With every tear and every line,
History's echoes start to shine.
In words that dance upon the page,
A glimpse of wisdom, a hint of sage.

So turn the leaves and heed the call,
In tales of wonder, we find it all.
For in the parchment, stories blend,
Revealing truths that never end.

The Quiet Scribbles of a Dragon's Call

In the stillness, a scribble sounds,
From deep within where magic bounds.
The dragon's breath, a whispered sigh,
Where echoes linger, never shy.

With every scratch, a tale unfolds,
Of fiery hearts and dreams of gold.
Through ancient caves, where shadows curl,
A dragon's spirit begins to twirl.

The parchment crinkles, inked with fire,
Each stroke ignites a deep desire.
For in the quiet, courage grows,
In whispered tales, the heart still knows.

With every breath, the story starts,
Binding together the beating hearts.
A legacy of realms unseen,
In quiet scribbles, bold and keen.

So listen close, to what they say,
In shadows deep and light's soft play.
For in the call of dragons, bright,
Lies the promise of enduring light.

The Cradle of Tattered Stories

In a nook where shadows blend,
Whispers of lore begin to mend.
Old pages dance in candle's light,
Cracked spines guard tales of the night.

Faded ink and trembling words,
Echoes of dreams, like captive birds.
A cradle weaver's gentle hand,
Stitching together a forgotten land.

Time flows slow in this hidden world,
Where magic and memories are unfurled.
Each sentence a spell, each poem a plea,
Breathing life into what used to be.

A tapestry woven with hope and fear,
Tales of lost wanderers drawing near.
In this haven of silent screams,
The cradle rocks with faded dreams.

Let the stories rise like morning dew,
Awake from slumber, born anew.
In the cradle, hear them sing,
Tattered tales of everything.

Tales Woven in Fire's Embrace

Within the hearth where embers glow,
Fables ignite and spirits flow.
Whispers arise from fractured logs,
Painting dreams amidst the fogs.

In flickering light, shadows entwine,
Crafting magic in every line.
Warriors of old and lovers lost,
Every word bears its own cost.

The flames are alive, a heart's delight,
In fire's embrace, dreams take flight.
Crafting legends both bold and bright,
Spirits dance in the deepening night.

A tapestry woven of ash and gleam,
Stories spill like a waking dream.
In the glow of the flickering light,
We find our way through the darkest night.

So gather close and share your plight,
As stories leap and take to flight.
Together we'll weave the tales adored,
In fire's embrace, we are restored.

Flickers of Ink-Drenched Memories

Between the lines where silence breathes,
Flickering ink like autumn leaves.
Memories spill from quills long spent,
Each drop a moment, each word a rent.

A journal bound in crimson thread,
Holds echoes of words once gently said.
Fingers trace the lines of yore,
Awakening whispers that time bore.

Ink-drenched moments of joy and strife,
Capturing shadows of another life.
Each phrase a flicker, a fleeting spark,
Illuminating paths through the dark.

With every page, new worlds unfold,
Adventures waiting to be retold.
Ink-stained fingers answer the call,
To breathe life into memories small.

So cherish the flickers, heed the script,
In pen and paper, let's not be ripped.
For in each line, a story waits,
Ink-drenched memories unlock the gates.

Charting the Unseen Winds

Beneath the stars, the night does sigh,
Searching for secrets in the sky.
With compass hearts and dreams in hand,
We chart the course through shadowed land.

The unseen winds howl their refrain,
Carrying whispers of joy and pain.
Navigating paths where few have tread,
In the silence, courage spreads.

Map the horizon with hopes unfurled,
In the dance of fate, we spin the world.
With every gust, a story blows,
In spirit's flight, our purpose grows.

The stars above flicker like fate,
Guiding sailors from beyond the gate.
Their twinkling ignites the fires within,
Charting the unseen, where journeys begin.

So lift your sails and dare to dream,
Follow the winds and let them beam.
In this journey, let passion guide,
Charting the unseen, we turn the tide.

Ethereal Whispers from Imagination

In twilight's hush, where dreams take flight,
The shadows dance, a ghostly sight.
Whispers twirl in a velvet breeze,
Carrying tales of lost decrees.

Laurels of stardust illuminate the night,
Colors blend, a surreal delight.
Voices weaved from threads of gold,
Secrets of ages long since told.

In every shimmer, a story hums,
A melody sweet, the heart succumbs.
Fables alive in the silken air,
Awakened, they weave a dreamer's care.

Amongst the thorns, a rose does bloom,
Crimson and fierce, dispelling gloom.
Imagination's kiss ignites the soul,
In realms where fantasy makes us whole.

So linger here, where whispers build,
A tapestry woven, imagination-filled.
Embrace the magic, the fleeting glow,
For in the heart, the dreamers grow.

The Tongue of the Dragon's Breath

In caverns deep, where shadows weave,
The dragon stirs, the night does grieve.
Fiery breath with secrets known,
In every roar, a timeless throne.

Scales of emerald, fierce and bright,
Guarding treasures hidden from sight.
Whispers echo, a tale unfolds,
Of battles fought and legends bold.

With every flicker of scarlet flame,
A world reborn, forever the same.
Mysteries dance in twilight's glow,
While nature trembles beneath the show.

Beneath the wings, a storm takes flight,
As stars collide in the shrouded night.
The tongue of ancient magic sways,
In tales of fear and joyous praise.

So listen close to the dragon's song,
For in its heart, we all belong.
Embrace the fire, let courage reign,
In the breath of dragons, lose the mundane.

Traces of Myth in the Embers

In ashes warm, the stories lie,
With every flicker, a soft sigh.
Myths awaken from slumber deep,
In memories held where shadows creep.

Fragments of lore in the night unfold,
Whispers of heroes, both brave and bold.
Through ember's glow, enchantments flow,
Carving tales for those who know.

The phoenix rises, wings spread wide,
A dance of fire, love, and pride.
Legacies within the light,
Glories captured, taking flight.

In the quiet hum of the burning wood,
Stories wane, understood.
Hearts entwined with ancient dreams,
In every spark, a world redeems.

So let the embers guide your quest,
In the warmth of legends, find your rest.
For in the glow, all truths align,
Traces of myth in every sign.

Etchings from a Transient Realm

In the twilight's grasp, where phantoms dwell,
Etchings linger, a magic spell.
Fleeting forms in a liquid sky,
Carve a path as the moments fly.

Between the folds of time's soft hand,
A realm unfolds, both strange and grand.
Ethereal whispers etch the air,
Secrets shared in a silent prayer.

With every heartbeat, a tale is spun,
Legacies spark beneath the sun.
Figures dance in a transient embrace,
Marking time in a dreamer's chase.

In the echoes of a world unseen,
Journeys taken, bridges gleaned.
Thoughts like ripples upon a lake,
In every breath, new wonders wake.

So wander far where the shadows blend,
In transient realms where dreams extend.
For in the etchings, life's truths shine,
A tapestry woven on fate's design.

Fantasies Adrift in Charred Whispers

In the forest where shadows creep,
Dreams entwine in silence deep.
Crimson embers float through air,
Each one holds a wistful prayer.

Moonlight dances on glistening dew,
Woven tales of ages new.
Whispers echo through the trees,
Secrets carried by the breeze.

Echoes fade into the night,
Fables born from purest light.
Time slips by, elusive friend,
Revelations around the bend.

Beneath the stars, a pact is sworn,
Fantasies from dreams reborn.
In charred remains of what once soared,
Hope and wonder, forever stored.

With every flicker, a wish takes flight,
In this realm where shadows unite.
Adrift in whispers, hearts ignite,
Creating magic in the night.

Ciphers Amongst Flickering Flames

In the hearth where embers glow,
Ciphers dance with tales of woe.
Flickering flames in shadows writ,
Messages lost in smoke a bit.

Each crackle tells of journeys gone,
Echoes whispering till the dawn.
Mysteries in fiery hues,
Unlocking stories, ancient clues.

With every flicker, lore unfolds,
Magic deep within the folds.
Figures leap and twist in time,
A language lost, a secret rhyme.

Fires rage, but hearts stay true,
In the darkness, we renew.
Ciphers glowing in the night,
Guiding souls towards the light.

Amongst the flames, we find our grace,
A tapestry of dreams to chase.
In the heat, we're bound and free,
Connected by this mystery.

The Hidden Scrolls of Celestial Battles

In the cosmic dance, stars collide,
Scrolls unfold where legends hide.
Heavenly scribes with quills of light,
Chronicles of an eternal fight.

Battles waged in silence vast,
Echoes of the ages past.
Celestial warriors in the fray,
In the night, they find their way.

Galaxies spin, destinies draw,
Mystic runes reveal the law.
In darkened voids, secrets swim,
Hidden truths, on edges grim.

With every stroke of cosmic pen,
Stories told from now to then.
Scrolls concealed within the flame,
Carving out the stars' own name.

Awake, O dreamers, seek the light,
In shadows thick, find what is right.
Celestial paths lead on and on,
In every heart, a spark - a dawn.

Legends Engraved in Smoke

In twilight's haze, legends loom,
Engraved in smoke, dispelling gloom.
Figures rise and softly fade,
Fables in the mist, portrayed.

Ancient fires burn with grace,
Storytellers in time and space.
Each wisp, a tale of old,
Lost treasures of the brave and bold.

Dreamers draw from ember's light,
Breathing life into the night.
In swirling plumes, a song unspools,
Teaching wisdom, the heart's own rules.

Heroes lost, yet never gone,
In the shadows, they'll respond.
Legends whisper, softly call,
Urging souls to heed their thrall.

Embrace the smoke, let stories rise,
In their warmth, discover skies.
Engraved in hearts, where dreams reside,
Legends live, and time abides.

Shattered Papers and Searing Dreams

In twilight's hush, the whispers call,
Old secrets lie where shadows fall.
With every tear, a story framed,
Yet none could bear the weight of shame.

The ink has faded, lost its grace,
Memories dance in a ghostly space.
Each paper shard, a mind unspooled,
In dreams we ache, by sorrows ruled.

Along the path of fleeting light,
Passions burned in the coldest night.
Promises cast to the winds of fate,
Forever lost 'neath love's cruel weight.

A heart that shatters, a soul that cries,
The grief that lingers, the hope that dies.
In each reflection, the truth resides,
Yet within the pain, new strength abides.

So gather shards, and mend once more,
Each bitter tale leads to what's in store.
For from the ashes, dreams can soar,
In the twilight between lost and lore.

The Haunting of Past Messages

Letters sealed with a sighing breath,
Words that echo like whispers of death.
In the corners of dusk, they softly brood,
A trembling heart, a wistful mood.

A quill once danced with passion bright,
Now dulled by shadows, swallowed by night.
Each phrase a ghost in the silent air,
Fading slowly, beyond repair.

They linger long, refuse to fade,
In twilight's grip, the truth is laid.
Past loves haunt like a fleeting dream,
In every heartbeat, a fragile gleam.

Yet from the whispers lost and shy,
New hopes arise, as we learn to fly.
For through the haunting, we will discover,
The strength within, a shining cover.

So heed the echoes of what was said,
Let not the past fill you with dread.
Instead, embrace the lessons learned,
As from the ashes, your spirit burned.

Messages Melting in Flame

In a flickering dance, the paper bends,
As time's cruel hand, its silence sends.
What once was written turns to ash,
Fleeting moments, gone in a flash.

Firelight flickers with tales untold,
Amidst the embers, the secrets unfold.
Each letter lost in the crackling blaze,
Leaving shadows, a soft, smoky haze.

With every flame, a memory fades,
Past whispers lost in scorching trades.
But warmth remains in a heart aglow,
While we remember what we used to know.

The pain tender, yet lessons gleam,
As ashes speak of lost dreams' theme.
Though messages melt, and voices tire,
From their remains, new dreams conspire.

So gather the warmth from the flame's embrace,
Let it guide you through time and space.
For in the loss, we find our way,
As hearts ignite in a passionate sway.

Riddles Woven in Ember

Amidst the coals where shadows play,
A riddle whispers, night and day.
Each twist and turn a secret told,
In the heart of fire, the brave are bold.

Woven deep in the ember's glow,
Are tales of joy and sorrow's flow.
In every flicker, a truth resides,
For the patient soul, the answer hides.

Time slips by in a dusky haze,
As riddles dance in the smoky gaze.
The courage found in thorns and gold,
Will lead you forth, as fate unfolds.

So chase the echoes of ancient cries,
Search for light in the darkest skies.
For every riddle is a path to tread,
In the warmth of fire, let dreams be fed.

In shadows' arms, together they twine,
Where past and future together shine.
Find your answer, let the ember guide,
In riddles woven, let your heart abide.

Forgotten Manuscripts in the Depths

In shadows dwell the tomes of yore,
With whispers hushed and dust galore.
Forgotten tales of magic spun,
Beneath the earth, their stories run.

Ink and parchment, secrets keep,
In chambers where the lost dreams weep.
Bound by time's relentless hand,
They wait for hearts that understand.

Pages yellowed with ancient lore,
Each verse a key to open doors.
In silence, they beckon the wise,
To unravel truth in disguise.

Mysteries glide on the air,
A scent of magic, faint yet rare.
Dare you seek the hidden light,
In shadows thick, a daunting sight?

Amidst the echoes, a flicker bright,
The glow of hope, a guiding light.
With courage drawn from the deep,
Awaken lore from its slumbered sleep.

Whimsy Scrawls of a Dreamt Wing

A feathered thought upon the breeze,
Whimsy writes among the trees.
In colors bright, the visions flow,
What dreams may sprout, and where they go.

Each scribble sings of flight untamed,
With laughter light and joy unclaimed.
The dreams of stars on paper dance,
With every line, a wild chance.

In twilight's calm, the stories gleam,
As moonbeams weave through each soft dream.
They flutter close, then drift away,
A magic moment, gone astray.

A flick of ink can change the fate,
A world anew, let's celebrate.
Through whimsy's lens, all life takes wing,
In a heart so bold, new hopes can spring.

So take these scrawls, a treasure found,
In laughter's echoes, joy unbound.
Let dreams be written, thoughts take flight,
As whimsy whispers into the night.

The Heartbeat of a Charred Page

In fire's embrace, a page once bright,
Now bears the scars of ancient might.
A heartbeat pulses through the ash,
Of stories lost in ember's clash.

Each charred line speaks of a tale,
Of lovers, heroes, ships that sail.
In smoky haze, the echoes call,
Of triumphs great, and of the fall.

Yet from the ruin, sparks can glow,
A flame of hope, in shadows grow.
For words ignited can still inspire,
And from the loss, arise the fire.

So let us heed the call of lore,
In ashes lie the tales of yore.
The heart beats slow, but beats it will,
With every line, our spirits thrill.

For from the charred and blackened core,
A wisdom forged forevermore.
In every burn, a lesson learned,
In every loss, a passion burned.

Inked Secrets in Fiery Realms

In realms where ink and fire collide,
The secrets of the past abide.
Flames dance wild, yet softly sway,
As stories breathe in bright array.

With every stroke, a spell is spun,
In whispered tones, the magic's done.
The ink flows deep, a mystic stream,
Flowing forth from a hidden dream.

In every droplet, cosmos lies,
Within the dark, creation sighs.
The fiery passion fuels the quill,
In realms of wonder, hearts can thrill.

So turn the page to worlds unknown,
Where inked secrets can be sown.
Each line a journey, passion's flight,
In fiery realms, all dreams ignite.

In ink do we find our truest fate,
The stories written by love and hate.
In fiery hearts, the words take shape,
Inked by secrets that will escape.

The Canvas of a Fabled Heart

In twilight hues where stories gleam,
A heart begins to paint a dream,
With strokes of courage, whispers bold,
A tapestry of love unfolds.

Each color spills a tale untold,
Of laughter bright and shadows cold,
In every fold, a secret lies,
Beneath the vast and endless skies.

With every heartbeat, brush shall dance,
Creating worlds where spirits prance,
In vibrant shades of joy and pain,
The canvas sings, it knows no chain.

And as the stars begin to spark,
The fabled heart ignites the dark,
Its tale woven through time and space,
An artist's love, a soft embrace.

So dip your brush in dreams anew,
With every shade, let courage brew,
For in the colors, life shall start,
An endless song, the fabled heart.

Veils of Echoing Echoes

Through tangled woods where shadows tread,
The echoes whisper stories said,
In veils of mist, they weave and call,
A haunting tune that binds us all.

Each step in silence, secrets hum,
The stillness thrums with thoughts undone,
Memories like leaves upon the ground,
In every crack, a voice is found.

They speak of times we've left behind,
Of laughter shared and hearts entwined,
In every echo, hope remains,
A dance of joy, a thread of pains.

The veils may shift with hues of gray,
Yet in the dusk, we find our way,
For echoes linger, bold and bright,
Guiding us through the endless night.

So heed the whispers in the breeze,
Embrace the shadows, learn with ease,
For every echo gently shows,
The heart holds truths the spirit knows.

Diary of a Dreaming Dragon

In a hidden glade, where silence swells,
A dragon dreams of ancient spells,
With shimmering scales and eyes aglow,
Its diary sings of tales below.

Each page a flight through starry skies,
Of worlds unseen and moonlit cries,
Where fire dances, and shadows play,
In dreams, the dragon finds its way.

With every word, a treasure found,
A tapestry of magic bound,
In whispered secrets, myths unfold,
Of hero's quests and treasures gold.

As night wraps round with silver thread,
The dragon writes, the dreamers led,
Through valleys deep and mountains high,
Its diary whispers, soar and fly.

So when you gaze at stars above,
Remember tales of dream and love,
For in each flicker, a journey's song,
Beneath the wings where you belong.

Codex of the Forgotten Flight

In ancient halls where shadows creep,
A codex lies, its secrets deep,
With pages worn and tales to tell,
Of daring flights through heaven's swell.

Each line a whisper of the skies,
Of travelers bold who dared to rise,
On wings of hope, through storms they soared,
In every heart, a dream restored.

Forgotten paths through clouds of white,
The codex glows with starlit light,
And in its ink, the past ignites,
A legacy of wondrous flights.

Through tempest's roar and silence sweet,
The daring spirit will not retreat,
For in the flight, we find our way,
The codex breathes, night into day.

So open wide the pages old,
Let dreams take wing, let stories unfold,
For in the skies, our hearts will soar,
The codex guides forevermore.

Words Enveloped in Flame

Flickering shadows dance and sway,
Whispers of dreams in the amber glow.
Each letter ignites, a spark on display,
Crafting a tale only embers can know.

Pages aflame with stories untold,
Echoes of laughter, of sorrow and cheer.
In the heart of the fire, new worlds unfold,
Burning through darkness, the light draws near.

Sentences twirl like a moth in the night,
Caught in the warmth of the fervent heat.
Words take flight on wings of pure light,
Carried through whispers of fate bittersweet.

So gather the ashes, the remnants of lore,
In the forge of the brave, where mysteries meld.
Each flame a reminder of what came before,
In the arcane fires, our stories are held.

Tattered Tales of the Celestial

Stars weave through the fabric of dreams,
Tales of the cosmos, tattered and worn.
Galaxies murmur, or so it seems,
Echoes of wishes on starlight reborn.

Moonlight whispers of lovers long lost,
A dance through the heavens, where sweethearts soar.
Through trials and triumphs, they count the cost,
Each constellation a map to explore.

Nebulas swirl in a colorful stream,
Cradle the secrets of how we began.
Beneath their glow, we awaken and dream,
In the vast universe, we find who we are.

Comets trail blazes of stories untamed,
Brighter than hopes flicker scattered in time.
Celestial wonders, forever named,
In the pages of night, they capture our rhyme.

So gather the stardust, the memories gleamed,
In each twinkling light, a story remains.
Through the tapestry of life, we are weaved,
In the heart of the night, our legacy reigns.

The Forgotten Flights of Ink

Once danced on pages, forgotten in time,
Ink spills like secrets from quills dipped in dreams.
Whispers of stories that clamber and climb,
In the echoing silence, imagination gleams.

Each droplet of ink holds a wish yet to soar,
Pages await to be filled with delight.
Paper reveals what the heart can't ignore,
Tales woven in shadows, concealed by the night.

Fleeting moments, like phantoms, they glide,
Captured in spiral-bound journals of lore.
From the depths of the past where memories hide,
Ink brings forth visions to long to explore.

So lift up your pen, let the ink take its flight,
Across fields of parchment, untamed and free.
With every stroke, let your spirit ignite,
In the realm of the written, find who you can be.

For lost in the clutter of time's grim embrace,
Lives a spark of creation, waiting to sing.
And through the forgotten, we'll find our own place,
In every ink flight, new wonders take wing.

Melodies of Burnt Leaves

In autumn's embrace, where the warm winds sigh,
Leaves drape the ground in a tapestry bold.
With each step, a whisper, as seasons pass by,
Songs linger softly, their stories retold.

Crimson and gold, a harmonious sight,
Rustling in time with the heart's gentle beat.
Nature's sweet symphony plays day into night,
In the cool breath of twilight, we find our retreat.

Echoes of laughter, of moments we share,
Wrapped in the warmth of the fading sun's glow.
Every leaf a memory, a moment laid bare,
In the melodies of change, our spirits will grow.

So dance with the whispers of rustling leaves,
Let the world fade away, in the soft evening light.
For in nature's embrace, our hearts find reprieve,
In the symphony woven from autumn's insight.

With each passing season, the melodies play,
In the heart of the forest, in friendship and love.
The burnt leaves remind us, in their own special way,
That the beauty of life is a song from above.

Evaporated Dreams of Flame

Whispers dance in starlit night,
Fleeting dreams take silent flight.
Embers flicker, shadows play,
Gone with the dawn, they softly sway.

Hearts once kindled, now turned to ash,
A fleeting spark, a blushing flash.
Laughter echoes, lost in time,
As dreams dissolve in morning's climb.

Fate's cruel jest, a twist of fate,
Chasing flames we can't create.
Yet in the silence there's a glow,
Of memories we've dared to sow.

Eclipsed by day, the night returns,
With every loss, our spirit yearns.
And from the ashes hope will gleam,
In this dance of a shattered dream.

So gather 'round, and weave anew,
A tapestry of vibrant hue.
With threads of spark, let fate entwine,
For dreams reborn in flame will shine.

Flickering Lines of Dragon Kin

In shadows deep where legends dwell,
The dragon's heart begins to swell.
With flickering lines of fire and scale,
They carve their stories in the pale.

Through mountain peaks and caverns wide,
Their whispered secrets cannot hide.
In every flicker, a tale is spun,
Of battles fought and victories won.

A kinship forged in sky's embrace,
In dance of flames, they find their place.
With every roar, the heavens shake,
Bound by the magic they create.

Through moonlit nights, their eyes aglow,
They ride the winds, two souls in tow.
Together strong, they face the storm,
With flickering lines, their hearts grow warm.

Their legacy, a burning thread,
In every heart where hope is bred.
So when the night falls, listen close,
To lines of kin, we cherish most.

Serpentine Scribbles

In the twilight's gentle hold,
Mysteries of the brave unfold.
Serpentine scribbles weave a tale,
Of heroes' fates and quests set sail.

Ink flows like rivers, deep and wide,
In words of dreams where shadows bide.
Each curve a promise, twists of fate,
A story penned, we contemplate.

With every swirl, a whisper calls,
Echoing through these ancient halls.
Beneath the ink, the heart ignites,
As scribbles dance in starry nights.

Hidden messages in every line,
A riddle's charm, a bond divine.
In serpentine paths, our spirits roam,
With every scribble, we find a home.

So let the ink flow, never cease,
In stories shared, we find our peace.
Through serpentine scribbles, we shall see,
The power in words that sets us free.

Ink-Drops in a Blazing Wind

In the tempest's grip, we find our way,
Ink-drops fall like tears of day.
Each drop a story, wild and bold,
Whispers carried on winds of gold.

Through the chaos, a melody calls,
Echoing softly through crystal halls.
In blazing winds, our dreams take flight,
Borne on wings of shimmering light.

With every drop, a memory stirs,
In the dance of life, our soul concurs.
Ink-drops painting skies with lore,
Opening paths to distant shore.

As the world sways to nature's tune,
We glimpse the magic beneath the moon.
In every swirl, a spark ignites,
Guiding us through the stormy nights.

So let the ink-drops fall like rain,
In blazing winds, we shall not wane.
For in their dance, we find our fate,
In stories writ, love will await.

Unraveled Stories in a Cinderscape

Amidst the ruins, whispers sigh,
Echoes of dreams that linger and lie.
Flickering shadows tell tales untold,
In the cinders, the mysteries unfold.

Once vibrant lives now turn to dust,
Yet in their ashes, there lies a trust.
The past entwined with the future's thread,
In the silence, the heartbeats spread.

Each ember glows with forgotten hopes,
Wandering souls, like ancient dopes.
A tapestry woven in fire and pain,
In the cinders, their stories remain.

Ghostly figures dance in the haze,
Through smokey veils, the present plays.
Unraveled tales in a world of light,
Reveal the shadows that haunt the night.

In the cinderscape, where time stands still,
The echoes beckon with haunting thrill.
Every flicker, a secret denied,
In their glow, the wishes reside.

A Symphony of Scrawled Secrets

Ink spills softly on a cracked page,
Words entwined in a silent rage.
A symphony woven with threads of night,
Where secrets whisper, hidden from sight.

Each line a promise, a tale concealed,
Beneath the surface, the heart is healed.
Tales of love, loss, and life's cruel twist,
In the margins, a world of mist.

The quill dances on parchment plain,
Drawing out joy, entwined with pain.
A sonnet of sorrows, where shadows tread,
In starlit letters, the past is fed.

Listen closely, feel the refrain,
Stories scrawled in the language of rain.
An opus born of forgotten fears,
A composition echoing through the years.

With each stroke, a heartbeat's cry,
Fragments of whispers loom nearby.
In the symphony of scrawled secrets told,
The magic of truth and dreams unfold.

Beneath the Wings of Ancient Legends

Underneath the twilight's gaze,
Whispers of legends from ancient days.
Beneath the wings of stories grand,
The dreams of many roam this land.

Time-worn tales in twilight's embrace,
Lovely shadows with a timeless grace.
Each fluttered wing carries the past,
In its fold, the memories cast.

As constellations guide the flight,
The echoes urge through the velvet night.
Legends soar on the breath of stars,
In their glow, the world isn't far.

From mountains high to valleys low,
Under ancient wings, the stories flow.
A tapestry yearning to be retold,
In the silence, the secrets unfold.

Together we weave with hearts in tow,
Beneath the legends, the spirits glow.
In the dusk of dreams, they intertwine,
In whispers of magic, forever align.

The Dances of Ash and Memory

In twilight's soft embrace, they sway,
The dances of ash in the fading gray.
Memory twirls with a delicate grace,
In the silence, a haunting space.

With each step, a story fades,
In shadows and smoke, the past parades.
Echoes of laughter, woven in time,
In the ash, the rhythms chime.

Embers flicker, a ghostly sign,
Of dreams once bright, now intertwine.
The dance of sorrow, the song of hope,
In the ashes, the spirits cope.

The swirling winds collect the dust,
Where memories linger, boundless and just.
In this ballet of time forever lost,
Each movement carries the heavy cost.

Yet within the sorrows lies a spark,
Of joy reborn, brightening the dark.
The dances of ash, a tender refrain,
In the folds of memory, we rise again.

Notes from a Tormented Quill

In shadows deep where whispers lie,
A quill doth scratch, its ink a sigh.
Against the void, it bends in pain,
To forge a tale of loss and gain.

It dances wild upon the page,
A spirit trapped in silent cage.
With every stroke, it bleeds the night,
A haunting verse, a flickering light.

Each word a ghost, a memory bright,
Of battles fought and dreams in flight.
Yet clarity is but a tease,
As shadows whisper through the trees.

The ink may dry, but sorrow flows,
In twisted paths where madness grows.
The paper bears a weight untold,
A story forged from grief and gold.

But in each mark, a spark remains,
Of hope reborn through ink and chains.
So let it write, the quill's true song,
For even darkness can't be wrong.

Ephemeral Scripts of a Flame-Hearted

In fervent hearts, a fire does blaze,
With scripts inscribed in passionate ways.
The flame, it flickers, but never dies,
Each letter dances beneath the skies.

To lovers' whispers, the ink conforms,
Creating tales of storm and swarms.
With every heartbeat, letters surge,
A symphony of souls, they merge.

But fleeting is the spark of day,
As shadows creep, they steal away.
Yet still, their warmth ignites the night,
A beacon bright, a daring light.

Across the pages, stories weave,
Of joy and pain, what we believe.
Ephemeral, like dreams that fade,
In every line, a spell is laid.

The quill, it dances, free and bold,
A flame within it, heart and soul.
Each stroke a witness to our fears,
While ink runs red like shed dark tears.

Yet as the fire wanes, we learn,
That love's fierce script will always burn.
Through fleeting nights and golden dawns,
Our flame-hearted tales transform the lawns.

Chronicles from the Abyss

From depths unknown, a voice does rise,
With haunted echoes, ancient sighs.
The pen descends in darkness' grip,
Each word a boat on shadows' trip.

The abyss whispers secrets tight,
Of creatures lurking out of sight.
With ink like oil, it trickles slow,
Revealing realms where monsters grow.

In every mark, a story spun,
Of treachery, of battles won.
Yet in the dark, foundation shakes,
As truths reveal what silence takes.

Each legend carved, a fleeting breath,
In history's grip, it dances with death.
Yet from the dark, a spark can swell,
In chronicles where echoes dwell.

Through ink-stained bonds, the shadows part,
Unraveling tender threads of art.
For every tale from depths we draw,
Awakens strength in each dark flaw.

So let them sing, the tales of pain,
For from the depths, our hearts shall gain.
A testament in ink and night,
In chronicles that seek the light.

Lost Letters to Mythical Beasts

A parchment crumpled, edges worn,
A tale of beasts, both wild and torn.
With ink, I pen my heart's deep plea,
To spirits roaming, fierce and free.

To dragons perched on mountains high,
And griffins that across the sky,
Fly fierce and proud, yet feel the pain,
Of solitude where dreams are vain.

These letters drift on winds of fate,
To creatures old beneath each state.
In dreams, I crave to see them near,
And share my heart, my every fear.

For unicorns in fields of light,
And phoenix flames that rise from plight,
Are guardians of secrets kept,
In woods of twilight where shadows crept.

But time doth twist the threads we weave,
And in the dark, we oft believe.
Yet hope resides in every scar,
With letters sent, I've come so far.

So mark this truth in ink and dream,
For every beast is not what they seem.
In lost letters sent, a bond will grow,
With mythical beings, hearts aglow.

Whispers of Forgotten Pages

In shadows deep, where tales reside,
The whispers drift like moonlit tide.
Old parchment cradles dreams once bold,
Awaiting hearts, their stories told.

Ink-stained voices, soft and rare,
Reveal the magic hidden there.
Through cobwebs thick, their echoes sing,
Of timeless quests and forgotten spring.

Once gleamed the light in eyes once bright,
Now dances gently, cloaked in night.
With every turn of page anew,
The past awakes, its spirit true.

A flicker here, a sigh from there,
To those who seek, the worlds laid bare.
Embrace the tales that haunt the air,
In every line, enchantments flare.

So wander forth, and never cease,
To find the fragments that will tease.
In whispers soft, the pages turn,
For every heart, a tale to learn.

Ember-Scribed Doodles

Upon the paper, flames do dance,
With ember-scribed, a wistful glance.
A fleeting thought, a spark of dreams,
In doodles grand, imagination beams.

With every stroke, a world takes flight,
In scribbled forms, bold lines unite.
A castle here, a dragon bold,
Where stories weave and laughter's told.

A heart that yearns, a mind that soars,
In every doodle, magic pours.
These ember notes, a fleeting thrall,
In whispered ink, we find our call.

So let the sparks ignite the page,
In every scribble, wisdom's sage.
Within the laughter, secrets lay,
In ember-scribed, we dream away.

As dusk descends, the doodles gleam,
Within our heart, they plant a dream.
So seize the moment, chase the fire,
In ember-scribed, we find our desire.

Echoes in the Margin

In margins wide, where tales are born,
The echoes whisper, soft as dawn.
A scribble here, a thought unsaid,
In fleeting phrases, secrets tread.

Each fleeting mark, a past retained,
In silent words, the heart is gained.
Through tangled lines, the memories flow,
In simple joys and tales of woe.

The little notes, both wise and kind,
Reflect the musings of the mind.
Laughter lingers in the space,
As written dreams begin to trace.

So pause a while, and take a glance,
At echoes here that made us dance.
In margins deep, the truth reveals,
A treasure trove, our spirit steals.

For every line, a life is spun,
In every mark, a chance for fun.
Through echoes soft, we seek the way,
In margins vast, we choose to stay.

The Keeper's Secret Scribbles

In twilight mist, the keeper dwells,
With secret scribbles, tales to tell.
By candlelight, the shadows play,
As whispers weave the night away.

With quill in hand, the magic stirs,
In every stroke, the heart concurs.
A hidden world of wonder waits,
Within the ink, a path creates.

Ancient runes and mystic signs,
In secret scrolls, the magic twines.
A cipher wrapped in moonlit glow,
The keeper knows the way to go.

So tread with care, and heed the call,
In secret scribbles, we find it all.
A flickering spark, a lore that's spun,
In keeper's mind, the stories run.

Through twilight's hush, the tales arise,
In secret whispers 'neath the skies.
Embrace the night, let wonder grow,
In keeper's heart, the secrets flow.

Tattered Pages in the Ember's Glow

In the silence of the night,
Tattered pages whisper low,
Stories flickering softly bright,
In the ember's warm, soft glow.

Dreams of magic intertwined,
With shadows dancing near,
Words like starlight, undefined,
Brush the heart, dispel all fear.

Secrets held in weathered seams,
Of heroes lost, and lovers found,
In the glow, they weave their dreams,
While time spins round and round.

Through the dark, a beacon gleams,
Illuminating ancient lore,
Of long-forgotten, whispered themes,
That call us evermore.

So let the pages turn anew,
With each flicker, tales unfold,
In the ember's gentle hue,
A magic waiting to behold.

Fragments of a Fire-Breathing Tale

Once upon a raging fire,
A dragon soared through skies of night,
With scales of gold and hearts of fire,
Breathing tales of endless flight.

In a land where secrets dwell,
Fragments of a legend stir,
Each word like magic, cast a spell,
Invoking dreams that softly purr.

Across the mountains, sharp and high,
Echoes of its roar resound,
Hushed whispers, like a lullaby,
In twilight's grace, they are found.

Through valleys deep, the stories wind,
Carried by the evening breeze,
As flickering stars, the fates aligned,
In every heart, they seek to please.

With every ember, tales ignite,
From ashes born, the fables rise,
In fiery hues, they shine so bright,
Fires of legend in twilight skies.

Echoes of Long-Lost Lullabies

In the quiet of the evening's glow,
Long-lost lullabies take flight,
Softly sung from ages ago,
Painting dreams in the starry night.

Whispers float on twilight air,
Carried far from where they roamed,
Secrets knitted with tender care,
In echoes, both gentle and domed.

Each note a thread in time's vast weave,
Binding hearts with silver lines,
In every sigh, a chance to believe,
That magic lives where love entwines.

Through the hush, the melodies drift,
Like shadows dancing in the glade,
As moonlight casts its silver gift,
In the dreams that sweetly invade.

So as you close your weary eyes,
Let the echoes cradle you tight,
For in each lullaby that sighs,
Lies the promise of endless night.

The Dusty Chronicles of Fabled Beasts

In corners filled with ancient dust,
Lie chronicles of beasts untold,
In every page, a spark of trust,
In realms where legends brave and bold.

With whiskers long and wings that glide,
Fabled creatures roam the night,
Through every tale, their spirits ride,
In shadows dancing, full of light.

From woodland glades to oceans vast,
Their stories weave a vibrant thread,
In whispered winds, the tales are cast,
Where every word a memory bred.

Where heroes whisper to the stars,
And dragons dream in skies so clear,
In lands of magic, free from bars,
Their laughter echoing, drawing near.

So turn the dusty pages slow,
Embrace the world where dreams reside,
In the chronicles that softly glow,
Let the fabled beasts be your guide.

Scorching Whispers in Ink

In the shadows, secrets creep,
Pages whisper, never sleep.
Ink like flames, it comes alive,
Stories sparked, they twist and thrive.

Among the quills, a ghostly sigh,
Murmurs dance and spirits fly.
Each line a spark in darkest night,
Fires of tales, a fierce delight.

Hidden truths on parchment lay,
Woven dreams, a bright array.
Ink's embrace, a tale to tell,
Scorching whispers cast a spell.

With every stroke, the world ignites,
Lost in realms of daring flights.
Flickering words, a vivid sway,
Inking moments, bold and fey.

Underneath the quivering light,
Scribbled truths in black and white.
Beyond the fire, the heart can see,
Scorching whispers, wild and free.

Silhouettes in the Ash Wind

Ashen figures dance and weave,
In the ember's soft reprieve.
Shadows whisper tales of old,
Secrets in the warmth unfold.

Through the smoke, a figure glides,
In the breeze, the past confides.
Memories swirl like autumn leaves,
Carried forth by what believes.

A tapestry of fading light,
Stories drift beyond the night.
Silhouettes in hues of gray,
Echoing the dawn's delay.

In the ashes, hope arrives,
As the quiet forest thrives.
Each breath stirs the stillness near,
Silent whispers, crystal clear.

Time stands still in twilight's glow,
Haunting winds, a gentle flow.
Silhouettes, they dance and blend,
With the fire, they find their end.

Pages Cradled by Fire

In the heart of every flame,
Pages cradled, none the same.
Softly glowing under night,
Stories birthed in flickering light.

Tales of heroes, brave and bold,
Breathe through ashes, yet unfold.
Every line a flickered chance,
In the fire, the worlds enhance.

Whispers flutter, shadows play,
In the warmth, they make their stay.
Holding dreams in smoldering hands,
Every ink-stained wish expands.

Mysteries glow in soft embrace,
Timeless realms, a sacred place.
Pages cherished, dance in light,
Cradled close throughout the night.

From the embers, visions spark,
Illuminating every dark.
Pages cradled, bound by flame,
In the fire, they call your name.

Scribes of the Scorched Realm

In the scorched realm, scribes reside,
With every letter, worlds collide.
Flames ignite their fervent play,
Crafting legends in dismay.

Parchment whispers, ashes speak,
In the fire, knowledge peak.
Such are tales of heart and dread,
Bound in ink, by passion tread.

Within the heat, their spirits soar,
Scribes of fate forevermore.
Chasing dreams that flicker bright,
In the dark, they find their light.

Against the blaze, their voices rise,
Scribing truths beneath the skies.
A dance of letters, wild and free,
In the scorched realm, they hold the key.

As embers fade, their legacy stays,
Written bright in countless ways.
Scribes of fire, bold and strong,
In their ink, the world's great song.

Ink Trails Through the Fiery Night

Beneath the stars, the quill doth fly,
In swirling ink, the dreams comply.
A canvas dark, the thoughts ignite,
Creating worlds in fiery night.

Whispers of tales long left behind,
Stitching together hearts and mind.
With every stroke, a story breathes,
In shadows bold, the magic weaves.

Through tangled paths, the memories chase,
Unraveling time with gentle grace.
The ink, it dances, wild and free,
Bound by the lines of destiny.

Though storms may rage and silence reign,
The power of words will still remain.
For in the darkness, a spark takes flight,
As ink trails through the fiery night.

A flicker of hope in the writer's hand,
Each line a thread through a woven strand.
The heart spills secrets, deep and true,
In the quiet hours, dreams come anew.

Lost Words in a Mythical Arena

In shadows deep where legends dwell,
The echoes of stories weave a spell.
Amidst the clash of swords and might,
Lost words linger, a fleeting light.

Each whisper carries a fated tale,
Of heroes brave and quests set sail.
In mythical realms where spirits roam,
Words become a wanderer's home.

With every breath, the silence falls,
As ancient magic softly calls.
In sacred ground where dreams align,
Lost words linger, forever entwined.

The arena glows with a mystic flame,
Where names are whispered, none the same.
A tapestry woven with echoes bright,
Forging destinies in the night.

Now hear the tales of ages past,
In the mythical arena, shadows cast.
Each heartbeat echoes with fate in view,
Lost words shimmer, waiting for you.

Shattered Silhouettes of Unwritten Lives

In corners dark where dreams once thrived,
Shattered silhouettes of lives contrived.
Each echo tells of paths unmade,
A gallery where hopes have swayed.

Fractured mirrors reflect the past,
In every shard, a shadow cast.
What stories dwell in silent sighs,
In whispers soft, where longing lies?

The canvas bare, awaiting brush,
With every heartbeat, a gentle hush.
Yet in the remnants, visions spark,
Unwritten lives, waiting in the dark.

Oh, how the heart yearns to create,
To weave a tale of love and fate.
But time slips through like grains of sand,
In shattered silhouettes, futures planned.

So lift the pen and dare to write,
In the twilight's hue, where dreams take flight.
For every life holds endless grace,
In unwritten tales, we find our place.

The Silent Madman's Journal

In pages worn from tales untold,
Lies the journal, strange and bold.
The silent madman scribbles away,
In every line, a mind in dismay.

With ink like shadows that softly creep,
He captures thoughts that refuse to sleep.
The madness echoes with cryptic rhyme,
Each word a puzzle lost in time.

A symphony of chaos, a heart laid bare,
In the silent whispers, vibrant despair.
Through labyrinths of darkened yield,
The journal's secrets become a shield.

Yet beauty struggles in tangled guise,
Amidst the madness, wisdom lies.
In every scribble, every tear,
A world is born, both strange and dear.

So delve into the silent night,
Where pen meets paper, and dreams take flight.
The madman's thoughts, a haunting view,
In the journal's depths, life is anew.

www.ingramcontent.com/pod-product-compliance
Ingram Content Group UK Ltd.
Pitfield, Milton Keynes, MK11 3LW, UK
UKHW021644160125
4146UKWH00033B/575

9 781805 635406